FOR YOUR HOME

KITCHENS

FOR YOUR HOME

KITCHENS

Rima A. Suqi

FRIEDMAN/FAIRFAX
PUBLISHERS

DEDICATION

TO MY PARENTS, LUCIA AND SALIM SUQI

A FRIEDMAN/FAIRFAX BOOK

© 1997 by Michael Friedman Publishing Group, Inc.

Library of Congress Cataloging-in-Publication Data

Suqi, Rima.
      Kitchens / by Rima Suqi.
               p. cm. — (For your home)
      Includes index.
      ISBN 1-56799-483-0
        1. Kitchens — Design and construction. 2. Interior decoration.
   I.Title.   II. Series
   TX653.S87 1997
     643'.3 — dc21   97-7241

Editor: Francine Hornberger
Art Director: Jeff Batzli
Designer: Jennifer S. Markson
Photography Editor: Wendy Missan
Production Manager: Camille Lee

Color separations by Fine Arts Repro House Co., Ltd.
Printed and bound in China by Leefung-Asco Printers Ltd.

1 3 5 7 9 10 8 6 4 2
For bulk purchases and special sales, please contact:
Friedman/Fairfax Publishers
Attention: Sales Department
15 West 26th Street
New York, New York 10010
212/685-6610 FAX 212/685-1307

Visit our website:
http://www.metrobooks.com

Table of Contents

INTRODUCTION

"No matter where I serve my guests, they seem to like my kitchen best." This popular saying, which for years has graced items as random as refrigerator magnets and needlepoint hangings, has withstood the test of time and turned into somewhat of a self-fulfilling prophecy. For today the kitchen is undoubtedly the most popular, and possibly the most important, room in the home.

Proof of the kitchen's popularity has been well documented. An official of the National Home Builders Association recently declared that a home won't sell unless it has a kitchen of excellent quality, with plenty of space and state-of-the-art appliances. That statement, in tandem with the fact that in the past twenty-five years the average size of a home has increased by six hundred square feet (54sq.m), means that certain rooms in the home—most notably, kitchens—have been designed larger. This increase in size is a direct response to an increase in the room's functionality.

Historically, kitchens existed only for the preparation of meals. In medieval England it was common to find the kitchen completely removed from the home, as a separate structure, thus containing all the smells and messes associated with that room. It wasn't until the sixteenth century that the cooking and living areas came to be housed under one roof, albeit with separate entrances. These kitchens, however, were often dimly lit and poorly ventilated, especially in the case of those found below the main level of a home. However, the kitchen as we know it primarily evolved in the eighteenth and nineteenth centuries when the range and precursors to the appliances we take for granted today, like refrigerators and dishwashers, were developed.

Some of the most progressive changes in the idea of the kitchen have occurred in the twentieth century. Kitchen design changed as a result of the changing role of women in society. Traditionally, kitchens were intended

Opposite: IN TRADITIONAL EUROPEAN KITCHENS, PLATE RACKS LIKE THE ONES SHOWN HERE WERE NORMALLY FOUND ABOVE A SINK WHERE THEY PROVIDED A CONVENIENT PLACE TO STORE AND DRY DISHES. IN CONTEMPORARY NORTH AMERICAN KITCHENS, HOWEVER, PLATE RACKS ARE ALSO DECORATIVE, DISPLAYING AS WELL AS STORING ATTRACTIVE DISHES.

for a sole cook, more commonly known as the housewife. As women moved out of the home and into the workplace, kitchens were slowly but surely redesigned and rescaled to accommodate more than one person preparing and cooking meals, or just grabbing a quick snack.

Above: THIS ROOM IS ALL ABOUT WOOD PLANKS, VARYING IN SIZE FROM BEADBOARD THIN TO LARGER SLATS FOR DRAWER COVERS. STANDING IN STARK CONTRAST TO ALL THE HORIZONTAL IMAGES IS A VERTICAL COLUMN THAT SEPARATES KITCHEN FROM DINING AREA. BLUE AND GREEN ACCENT THE WARM WOOD TONES OF THE ROOM, FROM THE WINDOW SEAT CUSHIONS TO THE STOOLS, AND EVEN ON THE WINDSOR CHAIRS THAT FLANK THE DINING TABLE.

Having more people working in the kitchen invariably led to more people lounging in the kitchen, and so the room evolved from a strictly utilitarian place to one that is more multipurpose and even surprisingly comfortable. Traditional boundaries were shattered and kitchens came to encompass the dining room and sometimes even the living room in a combination that was dubbed the "great room." Faster than you could say "a star is born," the kitchen became the center of family life.

That's an honor not likely to change anytime soon. For as quickly as the role of the kitchen has changed, manufacturers are just a step ahead with appliances to make working in this room so much easier, it will soon be almost a no-brainer. For example, at the time of this writing, at least one major manufacturer is developing voice-activated appliances, including ovens, microwaves, refrigerators and even washer/dryers. Electronics manufacturers have also embraced the kitchen, expanding and marketing their lines to include items like kitchen-sized televisions with built-in VCRs that mount or easily slide in under cabinets so one can watch TV or perhaps an instructional video while preparing a meal.

This is only a glimpse into what the future holds for the kitchen, and with the recent wave of technological advances, it seems that almost anything that can be imagined can be created.

Above: Fabric can hide a multitude of sins, as this space demonstrates. Because the left and right walls are so heavy with cabinetry, the designer chose to hang a gingham curtain from the sink counter instead of mounting cabinets underneath. The fabric adds softness and texture to the room and ties in with the colors of the floor and window treatment. In addition, fabric was used to line the inside of the upper cabinet doors to hide clutter stored behind them.

THE NEW COUNTRY KITCHEN

In the past, using the word "country" to describe a kitchen brought to mind very distinct images of handicraft, including do-it-yourself touches like frilly curtains, stenciled walls, weathered cabinets, and painted floors. Today, however, the country kitchen has grown up, and is no longer as much about adopting a stereotypical country style as it is about bringing the feeling of a weekend in the country indoors. Frilly curtains have been replaced by windows covered with shades or blinds, or nothing more than a wonderful view; stenciled walls are now dressed in tile; cabinets look aged, but not necessarily weathered; and floors are still painted, but with more sophisticated, geometric designs.

This new country kitchen retains qualities of the traditional, but is reinterpreted to look fresher by mixing in contemporary features. The most prominent of these features are professional quality or professional looking appliances, which have gained popularity in recent years. A large, stainless steel stove has become a staple in many kitchens, and as demonstrated on the following pages, can meld into almost any interior, thanks to well-thought-out interior design decisions, like choice of cabinetry and flooring materials.

Color also plays an important role, for there is no better way to bring the look and feel of the country indoors than with color. Bucolic shades of green, the warm red colors of autumn leaves, even pigments reminiscent of ponds, whether used on cabinets, painted floors or tiles, evoke the feeling of the outdoors. In a monochromatic kitchen, color is sometimes introduced in the form of collections displayed on open shelves or windowsills.

Perhaps the most obvious, and sometimes most challenging, way to bring the outdoors in, is to do it by literally using stone or brick for floors and logs of wood instead of planks for walls and ceilings. These are not always the most practical or affordable materials, but with a lot of determination (and perspiration) can be used to create a truly beautiful room.

Opposite: A RUSTIC FARM TABLE, WHICH DOES DOUBLE DUTY AS A SPACE FOR PREPARING MEALS—OR DEVOURING THEM— IS COMBINED WITH PIECES LIKE A PAIR OF WOODEN ROCKING CHAIRS AND RAG RUGS TO ADD A TOUCH OF COUNTRY WARMTH TO AN OTHERWISE STREAMLINED SPACE.

Left: THIS KITCHEN IN A 1960S HOLLYWOOD HILLS HOME WAS UPDATED TO THE PRESENT, WHILE RETAINING TRACES OF A "GROOVIER" ERA: COBALT-BLUE-PAINTED WINDOW FRAMES, TERRA-COTTA TILES FOR COUNTERTOP AND BACK-SPLASH, AND STIPPLED GREEN LINOLEUM FLOORS. THE CABINETS ARE SLAB WOOD PAINTED A FAUX GRAIN FINISH, WITH WROUGHT-IRON HARDWARE.

Opposite: THE SCULPTURALLY SHAPELY LEGS OF A SINK ADD A TOUCH OF WHIMSY TO A SMALL SPACE. BEADBOARD PANELING, USED HERE FOR BOTH WAINSCOTING AND CABINET LINING, IS TRADITIONALLY USED IN CONJUNCTION WITH MORE CASUAL MATERIALS, BUT WHEN PAINTED WHITE, WONDERFULLY COMPLEMENTS A MARBLE COUNTERTOP AND CONTEMPORARY FAUCET.

Right: A SPACIOUS, ALL-WHITE KITCHEN IS WARMED UP BY GREEN MARBLE FLOORING, SUNLIGHT STREAMING IN THROUGH A WALL OF WINDOWS THAT OVERLOOK A BAY, AND SOFT LIGHTS CLEVERLY RECESSED INTO A TRAY CEILING.

Above: A Victorian-style table, made of an ornate wrought-iron base and functional butcher block top, is the centerpiece of a kitchen that features wall and floor tiles more commonly found in bathrooms and the ever-popular professional range oven. Country elements abound, from gingham valances to a collection of animal pitchers on the windowsill over the sink.

Above: Vibrant green-painted cabinetry, packed with plates, mugs, and collectibles, boldly contrasts a stark white tile counter and accompanying cooktop, both mounted on industrial steel tubing more commonly found in restaurant kitchens. Here, one can eat from antique blue and white china while sitting on a modern classic, an Alvar Aalto stool.

Above: A pair of long plate racks above the sink serve two purposes: to facilitate drying, as well as storing dishes. Hand-finished cabinets bear an inscription of Roman numerals, perhaps commemorating the year this European country-style kitchen was completed. **Left:** Mismatched wooden chairs with colorful cushions, a pair of table lamps placed on a stainless counter, bamboo roller shades and a collection of wooden animals on the windowsill are all touches that make this a room to linger in long after a meal is finished.

Above: THE LOOK OF COUNTRY HAS ALWAYS BEEN ABOUT BRINGING THE COLORS OF NATURE INSIDE. HERE, CABINETS PAINTED ROBIN'S EGG BLUE WITH YELLOW ACCENT TRIM THAT MATCHES ADJACENT WALLS SET A LIVELY MOOD IN AN ENGLISH COUNTRY KITCHEN. **Opposite:** BRIGHT ORANGE MAY NOT BE THE FIRST COLOR ONE THINKS OF TO USE IN THE KITCHEN, BUT IT WORKS HERE. A WALL DECORATED IN ALTERNATING BRIGHT ORANGE AND STYLIZED FLORAL CERAMIC TILES PLAYS ON THE COLOR OF A FRENCH STOVE AND THE WARM TONE OF A HARDWOOD FLOOR. THE SOFT-TONED WOOD FURNITURE IN THE BREAKFAST NOOK REINFORCES THE EFFECT.

Above: A FLOOR PAINTED IN A COLOR TO MATCH CABINETS DISTRACTS THE EYE FROM THE CLUTTERED WALL AND COUNTER SPACES FILLED WITH KITCHEN TOOLS AND CURIOUS COLLECTIONS ON OPEN SHELVES. **Left:** A TWIG MOTIF USUALLY SIGNALS A MORE RUSTIC INTERIOR, BUT WHEN PAINTED A SHADE OF OFF-WHITE, IT TAKES ON A MORE SOPHISTICATED PERSONALITY AND ADDS TEXTURE TO THIS MONOCHROMATIC KITCHEN.

Below, left: IT'S ALL IN THE DETAILS.... A COLLECTION OF FRENCH APÉRITIF PITCHERS—INCLUDING TWO "SUZE" PITCHERS, WHICH PLAY OFF THE OWNER OF THIS KITCHEN'S NAME—SHARE SHELF SPACE WITH A MINIATURE MICHELIN MAN, A COLLECTION OF AMERICAN POTTERY, AND A STACK OF COLORFUL HAND TOWELS.

Below, right: A WALL MONTAGE OF MIX-AND-MATCH HAND-PAINTED CERAMIC TILES IS AN INTERESTING BACKDROP FOR A SLIGHTLY STAID BLACK CAST-IRON STOVE. THE SHELF BUILT IN ABOVE IT TAKES ON AN ARMOIRE-LIKE QUALITY DUE TO THE USE OF CURVED MOLDINGS, PAINTED GREEN TO COMPLEMENT THE TILES AND CABINETRY.

Above: TO BRIDGE THE STYLE GAP BETWEEN NEW, PROFESSIONAL APPLIANCES AND AGED CHERRY CABINETRY, THE DESIGNER OF THIS NEW ENGLAND FARMHOUSE KITCHEN CHOSE TO INSTALL A TIN CEILING BASED ON NINETEENTH-CENTURY DESIGNS. THE BACK-SPLASH TILES FEATURE WHIMSICAL KITCHEN AND COOKING-RELATED MOTIFS; THE LARGE SPOON WAS FOUND AT AN AUCTION.

Above: A GLEAMING STAINLESS TEAPOT MIGHT APPEAR TOO STAND-OUT NEW IN A ROOM FILLED WITH PIECES FROM THE PAST, FROM THE COLLECTION OF POTTERY ABOVE THE STOVE TO THE OLD WHEEL RIM NESTLED INTO THE WINDOW AND THE WEATHERED LOGS THAT LINE THE CEILING, BUT IS ACTUALLY QUITE AT HOME BESIDE A MORE OLD FASHIONED COUNTERPART.

Opposite: THIS RUSTIC KITCHEN IS NESTLED INTO THE CORNER OF A LOG CABIN SITUATED ON AN ISLAND JUST OFF THE COAST OF MAINE. THE LOGS THAT LINE THE CEILING, CABINETS, AND FLOOR ARE FROM GREAT ONTARIO WHITE PINE TREES.

The Sophisticated Kitchen

If one were to coin a motto for the sophisticated kitchen, it would be the French saying: *"Une place pour chaque chose et chaque chose à sa place,"* which translates to "A place for everything, and everything in its place." Here, the saying rings true, for the sophisticated kitchen is almost always completely built in. Cabinetry is flush with appliances and nothing sticks out from that one smooth plane, except perhaps an oversized professional range.

"Smooth" also describes these kitchens, which mostly feature smooth surfaces like stainless steel or glass, or highly buffed marble. In the sophisticated kitchen you won't find many textural elements like ornate cabinet doors. Most cabinets are completely flat for two reasons. First, the design aesthetic: since cabinetry usually takes up the most square footage of a kitchen, the look of the cabinetry will set the tone for the entire room. Simple cabinetry fits in with the unified, simple sophisticated look, and is easier on the eye. Second, flat cabinets are easier to clean since there are no nooks or decorative grooves for dust or food particles to settle.

Just as these kitchens are relatively void of decoration, they are also almost completely void of the usual kitchen clutter. Small appliances and kitchen gadgetry are hidden behind cabinets of stainless steel or perhaps pale wood. In some cases, oversized cabinets hide larger appliances like a washer/dryer or refrigerator. This type of design is ideal for loft living, where the entire home is a wide-open space, or for those whose kitchens are also their home office where employees and clients alike meet and sometimes eat.

Opposite: The challenge in this room is to find the appliances. Among the items cleverly camouflaged behind wood-paneled sliding doors are a refrigerator (to the left of the stove) and stacking washer/dryer (to the right). A cooktop and sink are set into the island, so the user can look out onto the rest of the apartment while preparing a meal. The pedestals of the island are covered in brushed aluminum.

Above: A freestanding troughlike structure houses both sink and cooktop, freeing up the opposite counter space for food preparation. Additional light is provided by a track outfitted with small halogens mounted underneath the cabinets. Cooking utensils are stored in a canister near the cooktop, and pots and pans hang from a rod that runs the length of the back of the structure.

Left: THIS KITCHEN IS MADE UP OF VERY SIMPLE, ANGULAR SHAPES IN THE CABINETRY, ECHOED IN THE RECTANGULAR EXPANSE OF WINDOWS AND THE SQUARE DINING TABLE, WHICH FOLDS OUT TO A LARGER SQUARE. THIN, ALUMINUM HORIZONTAL BLINDS COVER THE WINDOWS AND CREATE A SLEEK REFLECTIVE LIGHT PATTERN. **Below:** WOOD, MARBLE, AND STAINLESS STEEL ALL COEXIST IN A NEAT AND TIDY EUROPEAN KITCHEN. THE GENEROUSLY LONG CENTER ISLAND HAS A MARBLE TOP, MAKING IT SUITABLE FOR USE AS A PASTRY BOARD. THE ISLAND IS ALSO EQUIPPED WITH SEVERAL ELECTRICAL OUTLETS SO SMALL APPLIANCES CAN EASILY BE PLUGGED IN, USED AS NEEDED, AND THEN PUT AWAY.

Above: HAVING A COOKTOP SET INTO AN ISLAND IS A VERY UTILITARIAN DESIGN ELEMENT, FOR IT CREATES A CENTRAL PLACE FROM WHICH TO COOK SURROUNDED BY PREPARATION AREAS, AS SHOWN HERE. A STAINLESS STEEL HOOD PROVIDES REQUIRED VENTILATION AND MATCHES THE SLEEK REFRIGERATOR OF THE SAME MATERIAL. THE OVEN IS SET INTO THE WALL WITH A MICROWAVE POSITIONED ABOVE IN WHAT HAS BECOME A COMMON COMBINATION OF COOKING APPLIANCES.

Right: A FREESTANDING PORTABLE "ISLAND" WAS SPECIFIED FOR THIS ROOM SO THE OWNERS COULD HAVE THE FLEXIBILITY OF USING IT WHEREVER AN ADJACENT OR ADDITIONAL WORK SURFACE IS NEEDED, OR JUST AS A PLACE TO GRAB A QUICK SNACK. THE CABINETS ARE ASH VENEER PLYWOOD INSET WITH JUST ENOUGH GLASS TO MAKE THEM INTERESTING WITHOUT REVEALING TOO MUCH OF WHAT IS INSIDE.

Opposite: SOMETIMES THE SIMPLEST MATERIALS MAKE THE STRONGEST DESIGN STATEMENT, IN THIS CASE, THE PLYWOOD USED FOR THE SHARPLY ANGLED CABINETRY AND ISLAND. THE GREEN CABINETS ARE ALSO PLYWOOD, BUT WITH OLD FRONTS THAT WERE FOUND BY THE OWNERS AND PAINTED.

Above: THE OWNERS OF THIS KITCHEN LIKED THE IDEA OF INCORPORATING FRUIT SHAPES IN THE ROOM, HENCE THE BANANA-SHAPED ISLAND. MATCHING GRANITE COUNTERS AND BACKSPLASH CREATE CONTINUITY IN A KITCHEN WITH A LOT OF CURVES. **Right:** A LARGE PILLAR SERVES THE DUAL PURPOSE OF STRUCTURAL SUPPORT AND VISUALLY SEPARATING TWO DISTINCT AREAS OF THE KITCHEN: FOOD PREPARATION AND DINING. LIGHT FROM A LONE WINDOW SHINES UPON A GLASS BACKSPLASH AND A WALL OF GLASS-FRONTED SHELVES THAT PROVIDE OPEN SHELVING, BUT WITH ADDED FINGERPRINT PROTECTION FOR THE OBJECTS INSIDE.

Above: A problem with loft spaces—or a blessing, depending on one's point of view—is that there is no real distinction between one area of the space and the next. To ameliorate that situation, the architects of this loft added a circular, dropped drum to the ceiling that hovers over a portion of the kitchen area and the breakfast table. Panels made of glass and fiberboard (foreground) can slide closed to partition the kitchen from more formal areas of the home. Cabinets are ash, stained deep eggplant, countertops are black granite, and the backsplash is frosted glass.

Opposite: If it weren't for the sink and faucet, this room could easily be mistaken for an office instead of a kitchen, especially with the stainless steel cabinetry set off the marble floor and leather swivel chair. The low cabinetry allows for plenty of light to stream in from both the wall of windows in the adjacent living room and the area above.

Below: An extra deep marble sink is the star of this butler's pantry. The room has no stove, but does feature a small refrigerator to the left of the sink and a dishwasher to the right for cleaning up after parties. A water-friendly piece of limestone was set into the hardwood floor in front of the sink to catch water before it drips onto the floor.

Above: The angles of a custom-designed range hood lead the eye to the textural backsplash of smashed tiles set in a random mosaic pattern. The zigzag stovetop grid of the burners on this professional quality stove makes for a more even distribution of heat when cooking.

Above: THE CONCEPT OF THE "LIVING ROOM–KITCHEN" OR "GREAT ROOM" ENCOMPASSING BOTH LIVING ROOM AND KITCHEN HAS COME INTO FAVOR RECENTLY.

THIS ROOM MAKES THE CASE FOR THE "LIBRARY KITCHEN," AS IT IS A PERFECT SPACE IN WHICH TO ENJOY A BRANDY WHILE PERUSING A BOOK FROM THE NEARBY SHELVES.

THE RELATIVELY DARK MOOD SET BY THE CABINETRY AND BLACK APPLIANCES IS LIVENED UP BY CREAMY BEIGE WALLS.

Above: If the view into an adjacent room didn't suggest a home, one might think this was a restaurant kitchen. Indeed, almost everything in the room is industrial quality, from the appliances to the parts that make up the center island work area. The island is on wheels so it can easily be maneuvered to wherever it is needed most. Friends or family members can can pull up a stool to the counter to keep the chef company. The kitchen can be blocked off from the sun-drenched family room by pulling the folding screen closed. **Opposite:** For fans of the industrial looking kitchen, this room is a dream come true. Everything from cabinets to appliances to fixtures is either stainless steel or chrome. Diffused light flows in through a wall of glass blocks and reflects off the highly polished surfaces. Long, rectangular windows below the glass block wall push out to let fresh air in.

Above: Light wood tones with black accents are very Biedermeier yet the look in this kitchen is anything but. A glass-fronted cabinet for storing barware and stemware is conveniently located above a small bar sink set into a black granite countertop. A full-sized sink is positioned in the counter in the foreground, opposite the refrigerator.

Above: A SLATTED CEILING HIDES A COMPLEX LIGHTING SYSTEM OF FULL-SPECTRUM FLUORESCENT LIGHTS AND INCANDESCENT BULBS—NECESSARY BECAUSE THIS KITCHEN FACES NORTH—AND TIES IN WITH THE SLATS ON THE CUSTOM DESIGNED BENCHES. THE ARCHITECT CHOSE A FLUSH DESIGN FOR THE ASH-EDGED CHERRY VENEER CABINETS TO PREVENT THE KITCHEN FROM LOOKING TOO BUSY. TILES THAT LOOK LIKE VINTAGE ARTS AND CRAFTS PIECES BUT ARE ACTUALLY CONTEMPORARY HAND-PAINTED PIECES, LIVEN UP THE SPACE. **Right:** A PLACE FOR SERIOUS COOKING, THIS KITCHEN FEATURES NOT ONE BUT TWO OVENS AND A WALL FULL OF PROFESSIONAL-QUALITY REFRIGERATORS. A TRAY CEILING PROVIDES MORE FOCUSED TASK LIGHTING OVER A CENTER ISLAND, WHICH IS SET UP AS A PLACE TO PREPARE FOOD AS WELL AS SOCIALIZE. THE WROUGHT IRON OF THE BAR STOOLS COORDINATES NICELY WITH THE BLACK COUNTERS AND OTHER ACCENTS IN THE ROOM, WHILE THE RATTAN ADDS TEXTURE AND GIVES A CASUAL RELIEF FROM AN OTHERWISE SLEEK SPACE.

THE EXPRESSIVE KITCHEN

Over the years, the kitchen has evolved from a room used for solely utilitarian purposes to a room where people congregate—not just for cooking, but for eating and sometimes just lounging. As the functions of the kitchen have grown, the room has taken on a more personal tone, and as such is being decorated in ways that tap into the personalities of the owners, rendering the room, on the whole, more expressive.

Expressive kitchens reflect the passions of their owners. Collections are displayed either on open shelves or behind glass-paneled cabinetry. Works of art, or unusual materials like mesh screening, camouflage cabinet doors. Some rooms designed in the 1980s and 1990s are themed to look like they were wrought in the 1940s or 1950s with steel cabinetry, vintage linens and dining sets, and, in some cases, reconditioned appliances.

In addition, color, and lots of it, has found its way into the kitchen and designers are being anything but shy in the shades they choose. In some cases, color comes in the form of good old-fashioned paint used in newer, fresher ways. Decorative paint techniques like sponging, ragging, and stenciling are examples of this. For those without the time, money, or inclination to paint, color can come in the form of wallpaper that looks handpainted or stenciled, or in tiles that are available in almost every size, style, and price range imaginable.

Finally, whereas traditionally the kitchen consisted of appliances, cabinetry, and perhaps a table and chairs, many of today's kitchens are often part of a "great room" layout of one large open space that encompasses not only the kitchen, but also dining room and sometimes even living room areas. This type of expansion brings with it a whole new configuration of furniture and decorative accessories not normally associated with a kitchen, like upholstered chairs, bookshelves, and objets d'art.

Opposite: IT CAN BE A CHALLENGE TO FIND A SOLUTION FOR SECTIONING OFF ROOMS IN LARGE OPEN SPACES. IN THIS CASE, A FORMAL BUT FREESTANDING DOORWAY WAS BUILT INTO THE COUNTER SPACE TO SIGNAL ENTRANCE INTO THE KITCHEN AREA. THE BLACK ACCENTS ON OVERHEAD BEAMS AND CABINETS TIE IN WITH THE BLACK DOORFRAME, WHICH FEATURES SMALL, OPEN SHELVES ON EITHER SIDE FOR HOLDING VASES, STATUETTES, AND OTHER TREASURED OBJECTS. UNDERCOUNTER CABINETS ARE PAINTED TO RESEMBLE SHIRTS WITH BRIGHT RED COLLARS. THE LONG YELLOW SHELF TAKES A DRAMATIC DIP PROVIDING A NICHE FOR STORING COOKBOOKS.

Below: SQUARE TILES OF BROWN, BLACK, AND WHITE CREATE A DYNAMIC ZIGZAG PATTERN ON THE BACKSPLASH, AND THE SQUARE SHAPE THEME CARRIES OVER TO THE FLOOR AS WELL. RELIEF IS FOUND IN THE FORM OF RECTANGULAR SHAPES: ART HUNG ABOVE THE COUNTERS AND COLORED GLASS SET INTO A DOOR THAT SEPARATES THIS KITCHEN FROM AN ADJACENT BATHROOM. PLAYFUL HANDPRINTS PAINTED ON A FREESTANDING SCREEN REINFORCE THE SENSE OF FUN IN THE SPACE. **Opposite:** SOME SAY THE BEST WAY TO DECORATE A SMALL SPACE IS TO STICK WITH LIGHT COLORS. OBVIOUSLY, THE OWNER OF THIS KITCHEN DISAGREES. WALLS ARE PAINTED A BRIGHT COBALT BLUE AND STOCK CABINETS, WHICH WERE MOST PROBABLY WHITE AT THE OUTSET, NOW WEAR A SHADE OF TERRA-COTTA. CHRISTMAS LIGHTS STRUNG AROUND THE DOORWAY ADD ANOTHER FESTIVE TOUCH TO A LIVELY ROOM.

Above: A DECORATIVE PAINTER WAS CALLED IN TO STYLIZE THE OPEN KITCHEN IN THIS ART GALLERY. PARTICLEBOARD CABINETS GOT A WHOLE NEW LOOK, NAMELY A CUSTOM-COLORED THIN VENETIAN STUCCO FINISH APPLIED WITH A TROWEL THEN POLISHED TO BRING OUT THE SHINE IN THE PLASTER. THE CABINETS WERE THEN BUFFED WITH WAX. THE RESULT IS TRULY A WORK OF ART.

Above: IN THIS REMODELED KITCHEN, ADJACENT BREAKFAST NICHE, AND MEDIA ROOM, THE CUSTOM CABINETS ARE STAINED MAPLE VENEER WITH SMALL, SQUARE METAL CORNER DETAILS AND CUSTOM-DESIGNED DRAWER PULLS. THE LIGHTING SCHEME, WHICH COMBINES TRACK HALOGENS WITH A DECORATIVE CHANDELIER, GIVES THE OWNERS A CHOICE BETWEEN TASK LIGHTING OR MORE AMBIENT LIGHT. THE SCULPTURAL WALL SCONCE, MADE OF SAND BLASTED PLEXIGLASS AND PATINATED BRASS WAS INSPIRED BY A LOVE OF GARDENING AND CREATED BY THE DESIGNERS. **Opposite:** WHAT A DIFFERENCE WALLPAPER CAN MAKE. WITHOUT IT, THIS KITCHEN WOULD STILL BE BEAUTIFUL, BUT ORDINARY. THE LIVELY KITCHENWARE PATTERN OF THE CORAL-COLORED PAPER SETS A WHIMSICAL TONE IN THIS ROOM BUT ALSO DRAWS ATTENTION TO THE WONDERFUL WHITE CABINETRY WITH ACCENT TRIM MOLDINGS AND A STATELY STOVE.

Left: THE DESIGN OF THIS STOVE DATES BACK TO THE 1930S AND '40S, WHEN THE CONCEPT OF "COMBINATION RANGES" WAS FIRST INTRODUCED. COMBINATION RANGES BURNED TWO TYPES OF FUEL, USUALLY COAL AND GAS. SOME USED COAL AND ELECTRICITY. THIS STOVE HAS BEEN REVAMPED FOR USE IN CONTEMPORARY KITCHENS WITH THE ADDITION OF AUTOMATIC PILOT LIGHTS, BUT STILL MAINTAINS THE STYLE OF AN EARLIER ERA.

Above: THE OWNERS OF A 1930S CALIFORNIA HOME WANTED TO RESTORE IT IN KEEPING WITH THE ERA IN WHICH IT WAS BUILT. THE KITCHEN RESTORATION DEFINITELY FULFILLED THAT GOAL, FEATURING CABINETS WITH BRUSHED STEEL PULLS, VINTAGE APPLIANCES, AND ART DECO ACCESSORIES INCLUDING A BUILT-IN WALL CLOCK, A VINTAGE CAKE PLATE, A STRAW HOLDER, AND A COPPER PITCHER DISPLAYED IN A GLASS-DOORED, ROUND-EDGED, STAINLESS STEEL CABINET.

Above: THIS 1950S KITCHEN WAS PUT TOGETHER ON AN UNBELIEVABLY MODEST BUDGET. STEEL CABINETS WERE PURCHASED FROM FRIENDS WHO WERE GOING TO TRASH THEM AND PAINTED WHITE. THE TABLE AND CHAIRS CAME FROM A YARD SALE, AND THE FLOOR IS BLANKETED WITH ASPHALT TILES. FRIENDS LIVING IN THE WESTERN PART OF THE UNITED STATES MADE THE COLORFUL TILES ENGRAVED WITH WESTERN MOTIFS LIKE COWBOYS AND CACTUSES, IN EXCHANGE FOR A TRIP TO THE EAST COAST. LURAYWARE, A POPULAR DISHWARE OF THE ERA, LINES SHELVED WALLS AND CREATES A COLORFUL DISPLAY THAT COMPLEMENTS THE TILES. **Opposite:** MESH SCREENING HAS RECENTLY EXPERIENCED A RESURGENCE AND IS NOW BEING UTILIZED IN VERY NONTRADITIONAL WAYS. IN THIS KITCHEN, THE LOWER CABINETS FEATURE WOOD FRAME DOORS INSET WITH SCREENS AND THE PLUMBING, WHICH MIGHT NORMALLY BE HIDDEN BEHIND CABINETRY, IS INSTEAD ONLY PARTIALLY CONCEALED BY A SCREEN DOOR. THE USE OF MESH SCREENS HERE FUELS THE GENERAL COUNTRY PORCH FEELING OF THE SPACE WITH ITS VINTAGE TABLECLOTH AND RED AND WHITE FLOOR.

Below: APPLIANCES CAN BE DISGUISED IN A NUMBER OF WAYS. FOR THOSE WHO WANT PROFESSIONAL QUALITY APPLIANCES, BUT DON'T LOVE THE LOOK OF STAINLESS STEEL, THERE ARE OTHER OPTIONS. HERE, A BIG NAME REFRIGERATOR IS CLEVERLY DISGUISED BEHIND COPPER PANELS THAT FEATURE A CUSTOM PATTERN THAT SUPPORTS THE RUSTIC FEEL OF THE ROOM. THE COPPER OF THE REFRIGERATOER IS PICKED UP IN THE COPPER SINK BOWL AND RACK WITH COPPER POTS AND IS A NICE COMPLEMENT TO THE WARM YELLOW OF THE WALL-PAPER AND COBALT-BLUE PAINTED WOOD CHAIR.

Above: THIS KITCHEN IS A DESIGN PARADOX WITH ITS HEAVY, OLD, CAST-IRON STOVE WITH COPPER INLAYS JUXTAPOSED AGAINST AN AIRY LIGHT WOOD CABINET AND WALL-MOUNTED PLATE RACK. NATURAL LIGHT STREAMS IN THROUGH A WINDOW, CASTING SUNBEAMS OVER A LONG FARM TABLE AND PLATE RACK.

Above: ALMOST EVERYTHING IN THIS VERY BLUE ROOM IS AS HISTORIC AS THE HOME IT IS HOUSED IN, AN ESTATE DATING TO THE 1920S. THE BLUE AND WHITE CHINA IS A CLASSIC AND WIDELY COLLECTED PATTERN. FAIRLY CASUAL RUSH SEAT CHAIRS ARE GIVEN A MORE FORMAL LOOK BY THE ADDITION OF A PRINTED GOLD CREST, AND COMPLEMENTARY GOLD ACCENTS. WHITE CABINETRY AND FLOORING BRIGHTEN THE ROOM WHILE GINGHAM SEAT CUSHIONS AND A LIVELY CHECKED TABLECLOTH LEND A DECIDEDLY "COUNTRY" FLAVOR.

KITCHEN STORAGE

Storage. It's a universal problem. No matter how large the room, the amount of stuff acquired over the years will always expand beyond the amount of available storage space. The key in avoiding such overflow situations is good planning. While it may seem perfectly reasonable to design a space around the items one already owns, it is even smarter to plan ahead and estimate storage for items that will become a part of the room in years to come. Some claim that having well-designed storage will actually cut down on the amount of time it takes to prepare a meal, because everything needed will be in its proper, readily accessible place.

One such place that is continuously popular is the kitchen island. While the concept of the island didn't appear in American kitchens until about the 1930s, it now enjoys a can't-live-without-it status—and for good reason.

The island provides an extra work surface, and, in some cases, can be moved around the room to where it is needed most. An island can be used as a barrier to distinguish between food preparation and eating areas. In terms of storage, the island provides an easy access spot to keep items used on a daily basis, including nonperishables, or can be used to display larger platters, ceramics or heirloom pieces.

However, innovative kitchen storage is not just for the stunning pieces. Even the most mundane items need to be stored and can be situated in their own special places. Thanks to the new flexibility in customizing cabinetry, even the basic sponge has a hidden resting place, as does almost any item imaginable. Built-ins can be configured to contain spice jars, utensils, oil and vinegar bottles, and even stepladders.

Opposite: THE CIRCULAR BREAKFAST NOOK IS SEPARATED FROM THE FORMAL KITCHEN AREA BY AN INTERESTING CURVED DIVIDER THAT SHOWCASES A COLLECTION OF POTTERY. DECORATIVE SHELVES ON THE RIGHT WALL AND ABOVE THE RANGE HOOD HOLD LARGER BOWLS, WHILE SMALLER OPEN SHELVES ON EITHER SIDE OF THE RANGE MAKE SPACE FOR SPICES AND GLASSWARE.

Above: FOR A COUPLE WHO SAYS THEIR FAMILY AND SOCIAL LIFE REVOLVE AROUND COOKING, A FAIRLY LARGE (19 × 28-FOOT [5.7 × 8.4M]) KITCHEN IS NEEDED, AS IS A CORRESPONDINGLY LARGE (8-FOOT [2.4M]) ISLAND. AT ONE END OF THIS ISLAND IS OPEN SHELVING FOR POTS AND PANS, THE OTHER END, SHOWN HERE, HAS A GRANITE COUNTERTOP WITH BUILT-IN SLOTS FOR KNIVES.

SIX PULL-OUT DRAWERS WITH GLASS FRONTS PROVIDE STORAGE FOR NON-PERISHABLES AND OTHER FREQUENTLY USED FOOD ITEMS. **Right:** FOR A PROFESSIONAL COOK AND RESTAURATEUR, STORAGE SOLUTIONS ARE SOMETIMES FOUND IN THE SIMPLEST WAYS. HERE, CABINETS AT ARM'S LENGTH FROM THE STOVE AND ADJACENT WORK SURFACE PROVIDE SPACE FOR STORING VARIOUS BAKING SHEETS, CUTTING BOARDS AND OTHER FLAT, OVERSIZED SURFACES, WHILE A PULL-OUT SHELF IS HOME TO A STACK OF BOWLS, PIE TINS, AND TART FORMS.

Above: THIS UNIT REPRESENTS NUMEROUS OPTIONS IN STORING KITCHEN SUPPLIES. IT DOESN'T GO ALL THE WAY TO THE CEILING, PROVIDING AN AREA TO STORE DECORATIVE BASKETS. A COLLECTION OF PAINTED DISHWARE IS DISPLAYED ON THE UNIT'S NUMEROUS SHELVES. THE BOTTOM PORTION HAS DRAWERS FOR STORING FLATWARE AND NAPKINS AND ENCLOSED CABINETS FOR HOUSING POTS AND PANS.

Above: SOMEONE ONCE SAID THAT "WHITE IS ALWAYS RIGHT" AND THE DESIGNER OF THIS KITCHEN WOULD MOST PROBABLY AGREE. THE ROOM IS OUTFITTED WITH PLENTY OF CABINETRY AND FEATURES A FEW EXTRAS LIKE A BUILT-IN FORTY-BOTTLE WINE RACK AND ELEGANT SHELVING WITH FRENCH DOORS FOR HOUSING A BEAUTIFUL COLLECTION OF CERAMICS.

Opposite: ONE SIDE OF THIS ISLAND FEATURES OPEN SHELVING FOR DISPLAYING SILVER AND COPPER HEIRLOOM PIECES AND OTHER KITCHEN ITEMS. THE SHAPE OF THE TWO CEILING ARCHES IS MIMICKED IN THE CURVED ISLAND AND THE DECORATIVE HANGING LIGHT FIXTURES.

Above: THE DISCREET DRAWERS ARE PERFECT FOR STORING EVERYTHING FROM UTENSILS TO DRY GOODS, OR PERHAPS THE REMOTE CONTROL FOR THAT TINY KITCHEN TV. THE FOUR DRAWERS GIVE A BASIC SIDE-BY-SIDE, OPEN-CABINET STYLE A NEW LOOK, SOMEWHAT JAPANESE IN FEELING, AND ACCENTED BY INTERESTING BLACK VERTICAL PULLS. **Opposite:** AN IMPOSING WALL OF CABINETS LINES A STORAGE PANTRY IN A HOME DESCRIBED AS A CLASSIC GRAND COTTAGE IN MAINE. THE CABINETS RUN NOT JUST THE LENGTH, BUT ALSO THE HEIGHT OF THE WALL, WITH DECORATIVE CROWN MOLDING TOUCHING THE CEILING. AN IMPRESSIVE ARRAY OF CHINA AND STEMWARE IS EASILY ACCOMMODATED IN THE CABINETRY OF THIS HOME, WHICH IS NOW A BED & BREAKFAST.

Above: When this room was renovated, the challenge was to create plenty of room for storage on a budget that did not allow for full-fledged cabinetry. The solution: Metal shelving, as in the kind commonly found in stock rooms, sprayed with metallic gray automotive paint and an island with the same open shelving on the bottom with a granite top to match the counters. **Opposite:** Those with a passion for stainless steel will find that the range of this material is not limited to just backsplashes or appliances. Metal cabinets, most commonly used for hospitals or doctor's offices, are gaining popularity for kitchen use. But be sure you have the budget before falling in love with the look. Cabinetry of this kind is usually custom fitted and can be very expensive, not to mention high maintenance (think fingerprints!).

Below: A FREESTANDING CABINET OR ARMOIRE IS A WELCOME ADDITION TO A KITCHEN SPACE FOR SEVERAL REASONS. IT PROVIDES STORAGE, IN THIS CASE, FOR A COLLECTION OF VINTAGE CERAMICS. IT ALSO BREAKS UP THE SOMETIMES TOO-UNIFIED LOOK OF BUILT-IN CABINETRY, AND, WHEN PAINTED A BRIGHT COLOR, IS SURE TO LIVEN UP ANY ROOM.

Above: FOR THE KITCHEN IN WHICH EVERYTHING MUST BE HIDDEN, COMPLEX CABINETRY CONFIGURATIONS BECOME ESSENTIAL. HERE, FIVE SHELVES INDIVIDUALLY SLIDE OUT FOR OPTIMAL STORAGE OF, AND EASY ACCESS TO, DINNERWARE AND BARWARE.

Above: OPEN CABINETRY LOOKS ESPECIALLY ELEGANT WHEN STOCKED WITH WHITE CHINA AND CREAMWARE, CRYSTAL, AND A FEW WELL-SELECTED SILVER PIECES. THIS UNIT IS TRULY OPEN, IN THAT IT IS BACKED NOT BY WOOD BUT BY WHITE TILES. THE STAGGERED SHELVING OF THE CENTER SECTION ADDS VISUAL INTEREST AND ALLOWS TALLER ITEMS LIKE A PAIR OF CANDLESTICKS AND A PEDESTAL-STYLE FRUIT BOWL.

Kitchen Storage

Left: An island with built-in cabinetry is not a new concept. However, this extended island, with bench seating at the far end, features drawers and cabinets that look ill-fitted. This was very calculated, however, for the gaps between the units function as drawer and cabinet pulls (notice the cabinetry is devoid of any hardware). Units are differentiated by color. **Below:** The wonderful geometric patterns of these freestanding cabinets are emphasized by the curvilinear objects kept inside them. The upper units have no hardware and therefore give the illusion of being completely open when the doors actually have glass panels. Lower cabinets are a mix of traditional shelving with long, thin drawers perfect for storing flatware and linens. The grid pattern of the curved stainless steel chair backs completes the geometric theme.

Above Left: AN ELEGANTLY SUBTLE STORAGE SOLUTION IS FOUND HERE IN THE FORM OF A BENCH. THE TOP AND BOTTOM PARTS ARE HINGED AND OPEN OUT, REVEALING STORAGE FOR GLASSES, MUGS, BOWLS, PLATES, AND EVEN FLATWARE. **Above Right:** THIS PHOTO ILLUSTRATES THAT IN TODAY'S KITCHEN, THERE TRULY IS A PLACE FOR EVERYTHING. THE CABINETRY WAS CUSTOM DESIGNED TO HOLD A VARIETY OF PEDESTRIAN KITCHEN OBJECTS, INCLUDING SPONGES AND EVEN A STEP STOOL. INSIDE THE FAR DOOR, A SLIDE-OUT SURFACE HOLDS A HEAVY-DUTY MIXER.

Opposite: THIS KITCHEN DEMONSTRATES HOW TO MOST EFFICIENTLY USE A SMALL SPACE. NAMELY, PLENTY OF CABINET SPACE, WITH GLASS DOORS FOR STORING DISHES AND GLASSES, AND UNDER-THE-COUNTER CABINETS FOR POTS AND PANS. THE WARM STAIN OF THE CABINETRY GIVES THE ROOM A COZY, BUT NOT CRAMPED, FEELING. A RECTANGULAR WINDOW IS ALMOST HIDDEN ABOVE THE COOKTOP AND BEHIND THE HOOD, BUT PROVIDES AN INTERESTING VIEW FOR ANYONE WORKING AT THE STOVE.

SOURCES

Interior Designers

(page 8)
Jefferson Riley, architect
FAIA of Centerbrook Architects
Centerbrook Architects
P.O. Box 955
Essex, CT 06426
(860) 767-0175

(page 9)
Florence Perchuk, CKD
St. Charles Kitchens of
    New York
150 East 58th Street
New York, NY 10155
(212) 838-2812

(page 12, right)
John B. Scholz, architect
Scholz & Barclay Architects
P.O. Box 1057
Camden, ME 04843
(207) 236-0777

(page 13)
Elizabeth Speert, Inc.
Watertown, MA 02172
(617) 926-3725

(page 16)
John Silverio
RR 1 Box 4725
Lincolnville, ME 04849
(207)763-3885

(page 20)
Cann & Company
Boston, MA 02118
(617) 338-8814

(page 21)
Carole Hanson
White House Farm
Foster, RI 02825
(401) 397-4386

(page 26)
Bruce Bierman Design
29 West 15th Street
New York, NY 10011
(212) 243-1935

(page 30, right)
Totah Design
8170 Beverly Boulevard
Los Angeles, CA 90048
(213) 653-0416

(page 30, left)
Masterwork Kitchens
1 Hatfield Lane
Goshen, NY 10924
(914)294-9792

(page 32)
Lynette Hand
F. Kia-The Store
Boston, MA 02118
(617) 357-5553

(page 33)
Centerbrook Architects
P.O. Box 955
Essex, CT 06426
(860) 767-0175

(page 35)
Scott Marble and Karen
    Fairbanks Architects
66 West Broadway, Suite 600
New York, NY 10007
(212) 233-0653

(page 36)
Rios Associates Inc.
8008 Third Street
Los Angeles, CA 90048
(213) 852-6717

(page 41)
John D. Morris II
Architects/Land Planners
89 Elm Street
Camden, ME 04843
(207) 236-8321

(page 41, right)
Kuckly Associates
506 East 74th Street
New York, NY 10021
(212) 722-2888

(page 47)
Osburn Design
200 Kansas Street, Suite 208
San Francisco, CA 94103
(415) 487-2333

(page 48, right)
Lesley Achitoff
No Fo Decorative Painting
    and Plastering
216 West 18th Street
New York, NY 10011
(212) 807-0546

Karina Werner-Jakobi
Jakobi Studio
416 West 13th Street
New York, NY 10014
(212) 977-5142

(page 48, left)
Antique Stove Heaven
5414 South Western Avenue
Los Angeles, CA 90062

(page 50)
Candra Scott
30 Langton Avenue
San Francisco, CA 94103
(415) 861-0690

(page 56)
Dewing & Schmid Architects
146 Mount Auburn Street
Cambridge, MA 02138
(617) 876-0066

(page 57)
Mary D. Drysdale Interior
    Design
1733 Connecticut Avenue NW
Washington, D.C. 20009
(202) 588-0700

(page 59)
Douglas Truesdale Interior
    Design
86 Waltham Street
Boston, MA 02118
(617) 338-1156

(page 61)
Mary Drysdale
Drysdale Design
    Associates, Inc.
1733 Connecticut Avenue NW
Washington, D.C. 20009
(202) 588-7519

(page 63)
Edward Kozanlian Architect
220 East 60th Street
New York, NY 10022
(212) 838-4438

(page 65)
Barbara Barry Inc.
9526 Pico Boulevard
Los Angeles, CA 90035
(310) 276-9977

PHOTOGRAPHY CREDITS

Arcaid: ©Simon Kenny/Belle: 34 (Architects: P.Stronach/T. Allison); ©Willem Rethmeier/ Belle: 29 bottom (designer: George Freedman)

©Tony Giammarino: 26, 64 (Bruce Bierman Design, Inc.); 68 right

Rob Gray: 44 left (decorative painter: Lesley Achitoff-Gray, designer: Karina Werner-Jakobi); 63 (Ed Kozanlian, architect)

©Steve Gross & Susan Daley: 25, 54, 62, 64 right

©image/dennis Krukowski: 9 (designer: Florence Perchuk, CKD); 52 bottom (designer: Gail Pearlman, I.S.I.D)

The Interior Archive: ©Ari Ashley: 15, 45; ©Tim Beddow: 2, 22 right, 46, 52 top; ©Simon Brown: 28, 29 top; ©J. Pilkington: 17; ©James Mortimer: 18, 19, 42; ©Jakob Wastgerg: 68 left; ©Henry Wilson: 44 right, 67 right

©David Livingston: 14, 36 left, 40, 47 (Osburn Design), 48, 50 (designer: Candra Scott Associates)

©Maura McEvoy: 6, 30 left (designer: Joe Matta for Masterwork Kitchens, countertops designer: Steven Eickelbeck); 37 (designer: Bennett Bean)

©Peter Paige: 35 (designer: Marble Fairbanks)

©David Phelps: 56 top (courtesy *American Homestyle & Gardening* magazine)

©Eric Roth: 13 (designer: Elizabeth Speert, Inc.); 20 (designer: Cann & Company); 21 (designer: Carole Hanson); 32 (designer: Lynette Hand); 41 bottom (designer: Kuckly Associates, Inc.); 56 bottom (Dewing & Schmid Architects); 59 (designer: Geib Truesdale Interior Design)

©Tim Street-Porter: 12 top (designer: Roy McMakin); 22 left (designer: Suzie Tompkins); 30-31 (designer: Larry Totah); 33 bottom (Hodgetts/Fung Architects); 36 right (designer: Mark Rios); 38 (Smith-Miller, Hawkinson Architects); 39 (designer: Francisco Kripacz); 49 (designer: Richard Rouillard); 53, 65 (designer: Barbara Barry); 66-67 (Jeffrey Tohl, Architect); 69 (designer: Frank Israel)

©Brian Vanden Brink: 8 (Jefferson Riley Centerbrook Architects); 10 (designer: Jane Langmuir); 12 bottom (architect: John Scholz); 16 (architect: John Silverio); 23 (designer: Lou Eckus); 24 (builders: Bullock & Company); 33 top Centerbrook Architects; 41 top (architect: John Morris); 51 (designer: Kathleen Vanden Brink); 58 (designer: Robert Currie); 61 (designer: Drysdale Design Associates)

©Dominique Vorillon: 57, 60 (designer: killory design)

Index